# ÉMIGRÉ

## by
## Kathleen Bunyan Carlson

**ISBN**: 9798369746431
Front cover & interior photography by Vern Carlson
Editing & cover design by Gabriel H. Sanchez

Legado Publishing
Mission, Texas
2023

**Contents**

| | |
|---|---|
| Dedication | 1 |
| Introduction | 2 |
| Welcome | 3 |
| My Name Is | 4-5 |
| An Angel Came | 6 |
| Are Your Poems Truth | 7 |
| Furry Friend Lost | 8 |
| The Prompt | 9 |
| Thief | 10 |
| Authorities Found the Boat | 11 |
| *Sea Gull* | 12 |
| Travelogue | 13 |
| Émigré | 14 |
| The Suspect | 15 |
| Conquest | 16 |
| When I look in the mirror | 17 |
| Visit to the Festival at the National Butterfly Center | 18 |
| *Brown Longtail Butterfly* | 19 |
| The Bet | 20 |
| The Green Parakeets | 21 |
| My Makeup Foundation | 22 |
| Life in the Rio Grande Valley | 23 |
| *Grackles facing Off* | 24 |
| If You Meet Me in Tecáte | 25 |
| After Katrina | 26 |
| Dated | 27 |
| The Professional | 28 |
| The Daily | 29 |
| The Art | 30 |
| *Zebra Heliconian Butterfly* | 31 |
| Everyone | 32 |
| I Touched the Scars | 33 |

| | |
|---|---|
| My Son? | 34 |
| Poem | 35 |
| Yea, OK | 36 |
| Image | 37 |
| Query | 38 |
| *Giant Swallowtail Butterfly* | 39 |
| The Recollection | 40 |
| Tripping | 41 |
| Song | 42 |
| Next? | 43 |
| Vern Captured | 44 |
| In the Land | 45 |
| *Black Vulture* | |
|     *Warming in the Sun* | 46 |
| The Photo | 47 |
| Somedays | 48 |
| Addled | 49 |
| Adage | 50 |
| Aurora's Daughter | |
|     Loves Her Job | 51 |
| Dallas | 52 |
| El Valle | 53 |
| Gulf Fritillary Butterfly | 54 |
| Hammer Down | 55 |
| I Sent My Friends | 56 |
| I'm Free | 57 |
| If One Man | 58 |
| If You See | 59 |
| It Didn't Take Long | 60 |
| *Cardinal* | 61 |
| It's | 62 |
| Not Good Enough | 63 |
| Overwhelmed | 64 |
| Pleasant Poverty | 65 |
| Poets Against Walls | 66-67 |

| | |
|---|---|
| Post Poetry Reading Traumatic Stress Syndrome | 68 |
| Rescue | 69 |
| *White Winged Dove* | 70 |
| The Complaint | 71 |
| The Perpetually Pooped Pen & Paper Poet | 72 |
| Oración | 73 |
| A Note from Me-ow | 74 |
| Invaders | 75-76 |
| Final Request | 77 |
| Do You Know | 78 |
| Cynic | 79 |
| *Olive Tree* | 80 |
| Another Poem | 81 |
| World Renowned Photographer Commits Suicide | 82-83 |
| Tears | 84 |
| I Can Tell | 85 |
| Liberator | 86-87 |
| *Black-necked Stilts* | 88 |
| A Prayer for Elephants | 89 |
| Holocaust | 90 |
| A Poem for My Doctor | 91 |
| *Hummingbird* | 92 |
| His Anger | 93 |
| Husband | 94 |
| Pinky | 95 |
| *Moon* | 96 |
| | |
| **Special Feature Dance Poems** | **97** |
| Introduction II | 98 |
| The Dance Twinkies of Silvernail Road | 99-100 |
| Louisiana Men | 101 |
| Thoughts | 102 |
| Advice for Young Ladies | 103 |

| | |
|---|---|
| Chameleons | 104 |
| Leanna, Dance Teacher | 105 |
| Deep and Bright | 106 |
| *Rose* | 107 |
| I Have Watched This Rose | 108 |
| Why So Sad? | 109 |
| The Act of Dance | 110 |
| The Slink | 111 |
| *Aruba Girl in Saucy Red Dress* | 112 |
| A.K.A. | 113 |
| Upon Placing Second | 114 |
| When Trying | 115 |
| Dancing with Memories | 116 |
| Outro | 117 |
| Acknowledgements | 118 |
| Biography | 119 |

**Dedication**

To Vernon Marcus Carlson,
    my husband of 23 years,
        first generation American,
           born of immigrants
                from Sweden and Norway

# Introduction

Every individual who has ever lived in the United States once stood outside the Golden Door in person or as a dream in their forefather's eyes. This is a country peopled by immigrants. Even its first native settlers crossed into it from another land. They all deliberately left a place in search of a better life and another home.

I, however, was not one of them. I was dragged here. I was perfectly happy living in Aruba. My six-year-old mind could not conceive of a better place to be. Aruba is not called 'One Happy Island' for nothing.

I had a loving Mummy, a cute little sister, a disdainful older sister, a mysterious strong guy named Daddy, and a huge gray cat we called Big Puss. My favorite people lived down the street...my mother's sweet younger sister, her handsome husband, two adventurous boy cousins, and some cuddly old people named Madu and Padu. Plus I adored my first grade teacher Eufrau Lauretta at Peter Boer School.

The climate was perfect. The cacti were friendly. The boulders were just made for a child to climb up on and fall off of. Why would anyone leave such a paradise?

Nevertheless we left. I grew up.

The poems in Émigré are perspectives on some of my experiences from Aruba to Wisconsin to Texas, and many places in between. Please join me on my life's travels. Let us understand each other as people going on a long journey and as strangers coming to town. But let us go together.

**Welcome,**

**all my brothers**

**and sisters**

**under the skin.**

**My Name Is**

My name is Kathleen Agnes Bunyan
Januchowski Wells Carlson.

I am an American.
Call me Émigré.

"This flag was flown for Kathleen A. Wells"
certified George M. White, FAIA,
Architect of the U.S. Capitol,
on March 11, 1991.
\*\*\*

It has taken
over 200 years
for me to reach this point,
for me, the great, great,
great, granddaughter
of East Indian indentured servants,
African slaves, native Amerindians,
and English settlers,
from Guyana, South America,
to stand and receive
the Flag of the United States of America.
This flag, the parchment read,
was flown for Kathleen A. Wells.
\*\*\*
The people in the Capitol halls
wonder at my tears,
all of them
born Americans.
I touch the embroidered stars,
soft and bright
like the faces of the people

who come to my school for help,
people who have never stood
on the Capitol steps,
people who have no dream
of doing so,
all of them
born Americans.
\*\*\*

My family worked the fields for me,
worked the factories for me,
worked the shops for me,
though they knew they'd never see me.
My parents left their homes for me,
their sisters,
their brothers,
their fathers, their mothers,
their childhood friends for me.
One steamer trunk
and a suitcase for five
was what we took.
You see, it costs
to become an American.
It costs more than you think.
\*\*\*
I will put my certificate
in a frame when I get home
and place it on the wall
next to the one
of my naturalization
November 26, 1974.
So I will cherish the flag
as I will cherish the day
this flag was flown
for Kathleen A. Wells.

**An Angel Came***

An angel full of cheer and grace

came to soothe my anguished face

while I lay hurt in hospital bed

with tubes dangling 'bove my head.

With strong believing in her heart,

she changed my bed,

she checked my chart.

She urged the mending through the pain,

and made me understand the gain

of doing what the doctor said.

Time may forget the kindness done

but I'll remember every one

in these few lines of tripping verse

in praise of that dear angel 'nurse'.

*This is a universal poem. Change the subject of the lines to make it personal. Example, 'my brother's face', 'while he lay hurt', etc.*

**Are Your Poems Truth**

"Are your poems Truth?" she asked.
"Did you receive them
by revelation
like Moses on the Holy Mount?"
    For land sakes, girl.
    Poems are truth
    for the poet.
    God doesn't have
    to make a lot of noise
    for someone
    to write a poem
    about Him.

**Furry Friend Lost**

(a note of sympathy for someone who has lost a pet)

It's hard to part
with a furry friend
whose paws are wrapped
around your heart.
We understand.

It's hard to part
with a feathered friend
whose feet are wrapped
around your heart.
We understand.

It's hard to part
with a fishy friend
whose fins are wrapped
around your heart.
We understand.


etc., etc., etc.

**The Prompt**

Our doorbell rings.
I answer the door.
I see a semi-naked human being
crouched on a blue styrofoam tray
wrapped in cellophane.
I yell into the house
"We got another one."
My wife yells back
"Is it baked or crispy?"
"It's baked this time,"
I tell her. "Didn't
we order crispy?"
"Oh, just bring it in,"
she says. "They spoil
 so fast.
We'll have it
for lunch."
Lunch? I think.
No sooner?
My fangs are
already dripping.

**Thief**

Do surgeons
see blood
as a thief
trying to slip away
with valuable cargo?
The thief darts
and slides and furtively
hides the treasure
Life.

**AUTHORITIES FOUND THE BOAT,**
Headline in *The Monitor* newspaper
4/23/2016, McAllen, TX

at age fourteen
they had no fear
of death
the ocean was
their joy
it swallowed
them whole
two little boys
who cried out
in sad surprise
mommy… daddy
please come
please come

and the parents,
arrogant in their TV grief
stood on the beach
waiting for their boys
to come home
eyes sore from
scanning the horizon
hearts sore
from the self-saying song
guilty guilty guilty
waiting for children
to sail back into
their waiting arms
in visions seeing
grown men stranded
on a desert isle
finally returning
to mommy
to daddy
at last

Sea Gull

**Travelogue**

Palm trees waving in the breeze
the smells of sea salt
and frying plantains
remind me why we shouldn't
have left Aruba
for Wisconsin ---
Subzero winters enforced
by seven different kinds of snow
coats, hats, gloves, mittens, boots, pants
for every season except the one month
of pure summer there.
Now we live in south Texas
as close to Aruba as I could get
without crossing the Caribbean.

## Émigré

He was perhaps
age two or three,
a little refugee boy,
washed up on the shore
like a dead sea urchin.
No one claimed him.
No one screamed his name.
Did his family also perish
in their flight,
in their voyage
to safety and freedom?
Someone took a picture
of his crumpled little body
at final rest and still.
I cried for him.
Was this the enemy's child?
Surely someone had loved him,
yet no one had claimed him.
No one screamed his name.

**The Suspect**

Researchers said
cancer was caused
by an exchange of materials
at the chromosomal level.
Did it start in that damn apple
that Eve ate, that Adam ate,
that ran down through
the ages
to kill my mother?

**Conquest**

They found
bits and pieces
of her attacker
under her fingernails
under her toenails
in her mouth.
She fought him
with everything
she was,
the policeman said.
She squeezed her
vaginal muscles tight
after he finally got in
to force him
to leave evidence
and to eject him
from claiming her body
as conquest,
the disease
now making
him her spoil.

**When I look in the mirror**

When I look into the mirror,
this is what I see…
an aging weathered beauty
wondering what happened.
I had such promise…
I could have been a contender…
I tell myself I had no back-up
No one encouraging me
No supportive family, no wealth
It took such a lot of work
It such a long time
to work my way through
nine years of college,
through four years of graduate school
I just didn't have the time
I didn't have the energy
I didn't have the money
to be great
I just had enough to survive -

Vince said, "Yes, but you still ran the race
            and you weren't last."
He made me laugh
at my sorry self.

**Visit to the Festival at the National Butterfly Center**
Saturday, November 3, 2018

Queen butterflies
drink from a water crystal
in the grass…sip, sip and fly.
100 yards away
bulldozers churn
up and over
the soil
of the butterfly nursery.
I hear a baby cry.
Call this a festival?

A mesquite seed pod
caught in a spider web
turns red in the sunlight.

An etching
on a memorial bench
declares
"From your love
we grow."

Through the tumult
of human voices
cuts the shriek
of a cicada.
Visitors invade
the fields with fussing children.
The cicada gives up.

Does someone need a nap?

**Brown Longtail Butterfly**

**The Bet**

A guard at the state prison gatehouse
offered me a hundred dollars
(for what I hardly know,
but I didn't want
to get anyone in trouble)
so I looked deep in his eyes
and said 'Thank You'
with warm sincerity in my voice
and walked on by.
Me thinks the female guard smiled
a little smile.
Perhaps she'd won the bet.

**The Green Parakeets**

The Green Parakeets
are in stiff competition
for the Skreech of the Year award
in our neighborhood.
The Black Birds and the Grackels
better ratchet-up their yikes.

## My Makeup Foundation

My makeup foundation
sits in a jar
near my bathroom sink.
When I approach, it says
"Oh, no, not you again."

**Life in the Rio Grande Valley**
(a song)


Chorus and Verse One

We live in the Rio Grande Valley.
All the men here are handsome and smart,
The women are extraordinary,
And the children will capture your heart.

Verse Two

The cats and the dogs all speak Spanish,
But respond to the English for 'food',
The birds are multi-linguistic
And will translate when they're in the mood.

Verse Three

The valley is really a flood plain.
The landscape is rocky and flat.
The cactuses reach out to grab you.
We the people here like it like that.

Verse Four

Our marriages flourish with kindness,
Parents aren't harsh, but they're firm.
The whole family visits the doctor
To see what cures they can learn.

Verse Five
We span two countries with commerce.
We unite two cultures with love.
We pray for peace in our valley
And are blessed by Our Father above.

Grackles Facing Off

**If You Meet Me in Tecáte**
(a song)


If you meet me in Tecáte
underneath the cactus moon,
hand in hand we'll walk the hillsides
where the Pyracantha bloom,
soft the night birds will be singing,
soft our hearts will lift their tune,
if you meet me in Tecáte
on a gentle night in June,
if you meet me in Tecáte
underneath the cactus moon.

If you meet me in Tecáte
underneath the sagebrush sun,
side by side we'll skip the desert
where the salamanders run,
soft the coo coos will be singing,
soft our hearts will join their fun,
if you meet me in Tecáte
when the summer's just begun,
if you meet me in Tecáte
underneath the sagebrush sun.

*Chorus*

Oh, moon of June,
please take my tune,
straight to her room,
and bring her to me soon!

**After Katrina**

After Katrina,

the sky

over Wisconsin

looked like

vomit.

**Dated**

Reynolds Wrap —
*__Trusted since 1947__*

Holy Mackerel!
I'm older
than aluminum foil.

**The Professional**

He was such
an exquisitely
trained killer
people wouldn't
even know
he had chopped off
their heads
until they saw it
rolling around
on the ground
in front of them.

*"Hey, is that **my** head?"*

**The Daily**

Every morning I watch
The News,
I cry.

Every evening I watch
The News,
I cry.

What is happening
to my beautiful country?

**The Art**

the
art
of
the
quip:

**Zebra Heliconian Butterfly**

**Everyone**

Everyone
who
ever
lived
has
been
hurt.

**I Touched The Scars**

I touched the scars
on my mother's chest
where her breasts
used to be.
I was her nurse.
I was fourteen.
I wanted to scream
but I didn't.
I calmly applied the balm.
I calmly applied the bandages
and I kissed her face.
God, I wanted
to scream

**My Son?**

My son?
No. I would never give my son.
God may have loved the world
so much that He gave His
only begotten son,
but no, not I.
I would never give my son,
not for you, not for anyone in this room,
no, not for you or you
or anyone in this world.
You all are not worth it.
You all are not worth him.

**Poem**

an effective poem
can make
you scream inside

**Yea, OK**

I am sort of
      looking forward to death
      looking forward to the
           Return of Christ
      looking forward to seeing
          my mother again
     my first husband again
I am sort of
      looking forward to death
     sort of

**Image**

I can still see the photograph,
the sweet innocent face
the wide blue eyes,
a three-year-old
looking up
hoping for mercy
expecting none
as the stream of urine
splashed down on him.
He was the last child
to take shelter in the latrine.
He was the smallest and forced
to stand in the edge of sunlight
while the other children
stood in the shadow.
His mother had told him:
    "You must survive.
      You must live. Even if you never
      see me again, you must survive.
      I love you. I love you."…
    even as the Nazi soldier
    jerked her away
and the yellow liquid began to fall.

**Query**

In Aruba, people spoke
English, Dutch, Spanish,
French and Papiamento.
We moved to Milwaukee
where people spoke
English, Polish, German
and Italian.
What is all this fuss
about immigrants?
Go figure this figure,
ye multilinguistical purists,
'He rose to the bait.'

**Giant Swallowtail Butterfly**

**The Recollection**

She was kind to me.
Your mother was kind to me.
I was just a little boy,
just a little neighborhood kid.
      Tears came to his eyes.
      He was 65 now.
      He was telling us
      childhood memories
      at a high school reunion.
Yes, I remember your mother,
she was kind to me.

**Tripping**

My mind runs up and down the streets
of our neighborhood.
It stops at each house.
I ask myself - who else is dying?
      Who else needs the comfort
      of God's love?
People usually want to die in peace
surrounded by the people they loved
who loved them.
My mind combs our streets.
Who else is dying today?

**Song**

I am a poet, then a musician,
but sometimes poems make
songs of themselves,
and then I have to write them.
The song is in each word,
the words are in each note,
and then I have to write them.

**Next?**

My first husband
drove a milk delivery-wagon
pulled by horses.
My second husband
hammered
my wedding ring
out of steel.
My third husband
helped build
the Saturn V rocket
that took mankind
to the moon.

What next?
Who next?

**Vern Captured**

Vern captured

the shimmeressence

 of pink in his photo

of the Wandering Jew

flowering  in our yard.

**In the land**

In the land of grassweed,

we need a pricker picker-upper

that's not a cat, a dog,

a child or a husband.

Black Vulture warming in sun

**The Photo**

They were men, grown men,
old men, grandfather men,
yet they still wanted
something from their father
at age 106.
In the photo,
their faces leaned toward him
with love, with expectation,
eyes soft with hope,
waiting for the precious
"You are my beloved son
in whom I am well pleased."

**Somedays**

Somedays
I am just
chocked full
of poetry.
It comes
        squirting out
        spurting out
        spouting out
        spewing out
        surging out
        streaming out.
Somedays
not so.

**Addled**


After the first three notes
of the song,
I remember its name,
and by the fifth,
I remember all the words,
but I can't remember
who's President now.
I can't remember
the name of my first son,
if I had one son,
and which man
was his father.

## Adage

Mae West is credited
with saying
"If it's worth doing,
it's worth overdoing."
You know you've aged
when you follow
her advice
but find
the next day
you've lost
your capacity
to enjoy
the pain.

## Aurora's Daughter Loves Her Job

"I am an embalmer.
If I am the last person
to see you
before your burial,
I say 'Thank you
for your life.
I love you.'"

**Dallas**

a young Hispanic woman cried
as she gave a policeman
a six-pack of bottled water.
"I'm so sorry about your friend
killed on duty yesterday.
I don't have anything
to give you except this,"
she said through her tears.
He took the water with his left hand
and with his right arm, he hugged her.

It was on the 5:30 pm National News.

## El Valle

El Valle is a mystical/mythical place.
It is, yet it is not…here.
The spirit of El Valle glides
along the river banks,
caressing the plants,
stirring the animals,
enchanting the people.
We respond
to the turns of the river
with deep love.

**Gulf Fritillary Butterfly**

**Hammer Down**

If you know
you're going
to hit
somebody
hard
with your poems,
start with
a humorous one.

**I Sent My Friends**

I sent my friends
a love poem
capturing a tender moment
between them.
I was afraid they'd say
it was an invasion of privacy.
An invasion of privacy!?!
You know what's
an invasion of privacy?
holy spirit -
the one you receive
when you make
Jesus Christ your Lord
and believe God
raised him from
the dead.
Now there's
an invasion of privacy
for ya!
It's God in Christ in you
every day all the time
in every thing you do,
say or think forever.
You are never alone.
I complained to God
'Some hope of glory,
Father-Dude!'
Of course, He already knew
I was going to say it,
so when I did,
He was already
rolling around
on the floor of heaven
                                  laughing.

**I'm Free**

I'm free
from the fear
of tomorrow,
free from the guilt
of the past,
thank you, Lord Jesus,
you did it!
By your life,
death,
resurrection,
ascension,
you made me
free at last.

**If One Man**

If one man
of a certain race
can do it,
all men
of every race
can do it.

**If You See**

If you see
some small beige moths
fly around
      your grocery store,
you can bet your
      bottom dollar
that you'll be seeing more,
'cuz they'll lay
      their pearly eggs
      in your cupboard
      for sure!

**It Didn't Take Long**

It didn't take long

for the little reservoir

of cool inside me

to vanish

under the 95° sun.

I felt like fainting,

like vomiting.

Thank God

for Gatorade.

**Cardinal**

**It's**

it's really hard
to tell God
a joke.

**Not Good Enough**

The hymn goes:
    I love thee, Lord Jesus.
    I know Thou art mine.
    For Thee all the follies
    of sin I resign.
Here's my sacrifice:
I'm giving up sin
for you, Jesus.
Have I paid enough?
Am I off the hook now?

**Overwhelmed**

There are
so many poems
everywhere
I hardly
have time
to write them.
I feel my life
slipping away.

**Pleasant Poverty**

Some people like to reminisce
about the Good Old Days,
scrounging for food in the woods,
living in woodstove heated houses.
I myself did not find poverty
all that entertaining.

**Poets Against Walls**
July 30, 2019
Talleres Huitzilopochtli 2019

Writing Exercises

*What are people saying about my home that I don't like?*

Prompts:

*My home is not*
        filled with criminals, drug dealers and addicts.
        I am angry that you say it is.

*The border is not*
        to be used as a political tool, a divider of families,
        or an insult to America.

*El Valle is not*
        a barren, unproductive dessert
        of poor, ignorant Latinos on welfare.

*I am not*
        ashamed of the people of the Valley.
        I value them. I love them.

*What do I want the world to know about my home?*

Prompts:

*My home is* a garden
        where the riches of nature and
        the lovingkindness of its residents connect.

*The border is*
>the signature of two cultures
you can see from Space,
written by the gentle turnings of our shared river.

*El Valle is* a growing, living
>kaleidoscope of peoples.

*I am* pleased to live here.

## Post Poetry Reading Traumatic Stress Syndrome

I don't know when
the river
will flow
over my lips
like it does
over yours,
O you children
of the valley.
How many years
will it take
for El Valle y
El Rio Grande
to seep
into my body,
sink into
my bones,
and come gliding
out of me
like they do
out of you.

**Rescue**

The boy was trapped
in the Bougainvillea bush.
God told me loud and clear
"Lift him up."

So I did.

End of story.

White Winged Dove

**The Complaint**

Fighting vertigo is exhausting.
Body parts all
go their independent ways.
The brain pushes up and down while
      the inner ear free wheels
through hula hoops,
twirling around inside.
Lay down.
Take a break.
Close your eyes.
Nap.

## The Perpetually Pooped Pen & Paper Poet

Poems are everywhere.
I store little lined
yellow paper pads
all around the house
and in every room
so I can capture poems
as soon as they pop out.
In my purse
I have two pens
and one notepad.
Actually I am sick
with poetry research.
My stomach is churning.
Poems are every where.
How the hell
does God keep up?

**Oración**

Dios,
por favor
bendiga
nuestro
valle.
Gracias
con todo
mi
corazón.

**A Note from Me-ow**

Yes, dear,
we do have
to talk to humans.
They cannot
understand
the nuances
of CatSlam.
Nor do they
have the requisite
body parts
(i.e., tails, pupil control,
back arch)
to convey meaning
without verbalization,
poor things.

        Love,
                Nugget

**Invaders**

the man
face down
stretched out in the water
was young
wiry in build
seemed like he was
still reaching for the river bank
rocking to the rhythm of the water.
on his back, under his shirt,
was a lump
hard to make out
Oh, a child, a young child's head,
dark curly hair,
held to his back
under his shirt.

the woman said they'd walked
over 800 miles to get to
the Rio Grande River,
the five of them -
mother, father, three children.
She told us that she
and the two older children
could swim enough to cross
but the baby couldn't.
Papi put her in his shirt
on his back to swim her across
'Hold on tight,' he told her, 'hold on'.

What did the father feel
when he knew he couldn't make it across,
when the water started choking him,
when the weight of his baby bore him down?

Did he hear the baby crying, 'Papi, Papi?'
Did he curse the river and
the desperate ugly life they'd left?
Did he beg God to spare his child
even if He couldn't save him?

*Papi... Papi*!

**Final Request**

To those of you who were
      going to be nice
      to us old codgers
      before we died,
To all teenagers and young people:
      think of ways to get rid of
      all the useless plastic in the world,
      for example:
            Make all the plastic
            into a rocket
            that fuels itself
            on plastic and
            launch it into the sun.
Got any better ideas?

**Do You Know**

Do you know
what happens
when the heart
of a home dies?
The rest of the body
flops around
for a while
and when the parts realize
the heart is not
coming back,
they stop flopping
and go looking
for another heart.
That's what happened
when our mother died.
We screamed and cried
and flopped around
for a while
and them we left the house
because there was
no heart there,
no home there,
no love there.
We went looking
but we never found
a love like hers again.

**Cynic**

I am looking at love today.
I want to understand love.

*For God so loved...*
      'so' - way far out,
      beyond the normal,
      to the extreme limit...

People say loving us
cost God his only begotten son.
Is that accurate?
He resurrected Jesus Christ as soon
as he had finished the job.
He had a living son again.

It didn't cost God anything.

Olive Tree

**Another Poem**


I want to write a poem
about this article and photo
in the newspaper




but this is not the poem.
This is the set up to the poem:

Water Cat

## World Renowned Photographer Commits Suicide -

*The Planet Times*

I know I'm just a hyena,
so I don't have any thing
to boast about, and I of all animals
shouldn't make judgments,
but will you take a look
at that guy over there?

He's taking photos of a child,
a child dying of hunger and thirst,
a child.
He's not even getting close enough
to help the poor kid.
The boy is so emaciated that
his head is the biggest
part of his body,
so heavy he can't
even hold it up.
He's all hunched over,
arms and legs like
little sticks,
the bulbous head
down on the ground.

Oh, Lord, he's calling
for his mother.

People say hyenas
have no ethics, no heart.
At least I'd drag the kid
home to feed my family,

(well, not this one -
too skinny,
not enough flesh
to make the trip worthwhile).

But not this guy, this photographer,
He's in it for the money,
the prestige, the awards.
He doesn't give a rip
about a dying African child.
God, do something.
The kid is almost dead.
There's no Christ in sight.

How can this man stand himself?
I don't think even a hyena
would lick him.

**Tears**

Tears ran down
the policeman's face.
He was armored and shielded,
locked and loaded,
ready to fire, to maim, to kill.
The Holy Night song rang
from the choir
out into the frenzied Mall air.
The stars were
brightly shining.
All paused.
All listened.
Tears ran down
the policeman's face.

Capitol Court Mall,
Milwaukee, 1985

## I Can Tell

I can tell
that the people
wading across the river
are strong.
Their eyes are hard
focussed on their goal -
reaching the United States.
They have walked
1100 miles and paid
thousands of dollars
to cross this river.
There is no
"I guess I'll give up now"
on their mouths
or in their eyes.

**Liberator**


When I returned to my car
 after a meeting at the local Barnes and Noble Bookstore,
 I was horrified to see a huge butterfly on the floor,
wedged in the channel between the driver's side door
and the driver's seat.
I figured the wingspan to be about eight inches,
black and white and orange and incredibly fuzzy.
I knew I was not about to touch that thing.
Right away I looked around the parking lot for help.
Man…woman…young…old…Nope, no one.
I crept back into the B&N and scanned for potential saviors.
I saw a well-built man, late twenties/early thirties,
about 6 ft. tall, scanning magazines.
Immediately I knew he was the one.
He was wearing Army fatigues and heavy tan boots.
I scurried over to him and said,
"Excuse me , sir. You look like a big strong man.
Are you afraid of bugs?"
 "No", he said, "but I'm looking at someone who is."
He laughed. I smiled faintly.
"Where is the bug?" he asked.
I led him out to my car, opened
the driver's side door and pointed
to the monster butterfly.
"Um, that is a big one," he said.
He reached down to pick it up but his hand
was too big for the narrow channel.
"Maybe I can get to it from behind the seat."
I opened the side door for him.
He came around
and reached it from the back.
He squeezed it with a pinch hold and took it out.

I recoiled and made the appropriate girl sounds.
"It's dead", he said and placed it in a nearby stone planter.
I thanked him profusely and as he walked back
into the B&N, I realized I had just
pushed Women's Lib back 20 years.

**Black-necked Stilts**

## A Prayer for Elephants

O, God, my Father,
please protect these elephants,
the ones I see on this calendar,
bathing in a sunlit pool of dust,
throwing it with joy
over their heads and backs.
Protect them, O God,
where ever they are
in the world
doing what elephants do.
We killed off so many
bison here, there were hardly
enough left to restart
the species.
We Americans were greedy,
and ignorant and arrogant.
But you Africans and Indians -
look at our bad example
and learn.
Don't kill off all of your elephants.
Don't be greedy, and ignorant
and arrogant
like us.

**Holocaust**

Definition: the deliberate, systematic murder of people to prove one's superiority, to seize lands and goods, to destroy races, religions and cultures, to avenge perceived wrongs.

> "What we have seen,
> human hearts
> were not meant
> to see.
> What was done to us,
> human hands
> were not imagined
> to do."

*~Ukrainian Holocaust Survivor*
*~Russian Holocaust Survivor*
*~German Holocaust Survivor*
*~Jewish Holocaust Survivor*
*~American Holocaust Survivor*
*~Darfur Holocaust Survivor*
*~Australian Holocaust Survivor*
*~Japanese Holocaust Survivor*
*~Chinese Holocaust Survivor*
*~Tutu Holocaust Survivor*
*~Maori Holocaust Survivor*
*~Malaysian Holocaust Survivor*
*~Aztec Holocaust Survivor\**
*~Pygmy Holocaust Survivor*

and so on, and so further,
and so more

\*There were none.

## A Poem for My Doctor

You fixed my heart
so it ran right.
It has not
skipped a beat
nor cheated me
of a second of life
nor deprived me
of a ray of light
since you
made my heart
run right.

Thank you.

**Hummingbird**

**His Anger**

        the voice of the man
           telling the story
      the voice of the boy
              experiencing the story


His anger covered my mother
like a thick black cloud
swelling and swallowing her
in his hate.
Peeping from behind her skirts,
I saw the anger spew
out of the shopkeeper.
She just didn't know
the word in English, mister,
the word for the thing she wanted
to ask for her family.
I was just a little boy.
It made me afraid
to see this White man
belching out malevolence
out of his eyes, his mouth
over my little mama.
Would he try to hurt her
Would he try to kill her?
She just didn't
know the word, gringo.
Don't hurt my mama
I silently cried out.
I was just a little boy then
but now I am a man.
I am a man and I remember.

## Husband

Husband,
I'm ready
to have you
do for me
whatever you
thought you were
going to do
before you
lost track
of doing
whatever
you thought
you were
going to
do…
going…
…doing
thtt

**Pinky**

it is abundantly clear
in the Silverado commercial,
the one with all the truck's
panoramic views,
that that father
does not want
that young man
doing to his daughter
what he did
with another man's daughter
to bring forth
the girl sitting
in the truck's back seat,
who with the pinky finger
of her tiny infant hand
ripped his heart right
out of his chest
and never gave it back.

Moon

# SURPRISE FEATURE

# DANCE POEMS

## Introduction II

Dancing is very popular in the midwest where I grew up. People living here come from Europe, Central and South America, Middle East, Asia, Africa, the Caribbean, and the Mediterranean.

Every culture celebrates life with festivals of food, crafts, clothing, song and dance. Hardly a month goes by that some group isn't engaged in the joy of their heritage and inviting others to come and eat and dance with them.

The world of ballroom dance adds a different dimension. In this world, dancers strive for perfection in technique, form, costume and performance. A Tango must not just look like a Tango. It must feel like a Tango and draw watchers into its heady romantic web. And there lies the danger...

## The Dance Twinkies of Silvernail Road

Late in the morning
on little dance feet
into the studio
the Dance Twinkies leap.
They scatter their dance dust
all through the day.
With romance and magic
the Dance Twinkies play.
They first charm the honey
right out of your heart
and so with your money
you're eager to part.
They tickle your cash
out of wallet and purse
with a combo of chutzpa,
music and verse.
They promise affection,
 excitement, desire.
They brighten your day
with the flash of their fire.
They ask hours and dollars
which you gladly give -
Life without Twinkies
is so dull to live.
With each waltz and tango,
with cha cha cha, too,
with eastern swing,
western swing,
pasa doubloo,
they strengthen their spell,
make you hungry for more,
then turn off the music
and show you the door.

With the sadness of parting
in mellow moonlight
we call 'good night,
little Twinkies,
good night'.

**Louisiana Men**

Louisiana men
came to our town,
their eyes the softness
of a Southern dawn.
Louisiana men
knocked at my door,
hinting at love
yet asking for more.
Louisiana men
waltzed into my heart
and lit up a place
left empty and dark
by betrayal of trust,
then waltzed out again
but left music and light,
Louisiana men.

**Thoughts**

I was hoping
I wouldn't start
loving you,
dance teacher.
If you leave here,
please don't go
without saying
goodbye.
Don't wrench yourself
out of my heart
and life
without giving me
the chance
to cry and mourn
for at least
a couple of hours
before I move on
to the next
dancing guy.

**Advice for
Young Ladies:**

Never follow a man
who follows you
for
he obviously doesn't know
where he's going.

**Chameleons**

It was interesting to watch the dance -
Before us, the dowagers,
they were teachers, confident,
charming young males,
professional dancers,
off limits due to age
and social convention.
Before these young girls, their peers,
their confidence vanished
they became boys again 19 and 21
subject to rejection
fearful of pimples,
longing for acceptance
a smile, a gentle lift of the eye.
We never reject them
(we would dance with
anything that hath breath)
but these girls have options.

**Leanna, Dance Teacher**

Her red hair
floats upon the spume
the river casts
into the night sky.
The light from
the electric bobber
paints her face
with softly moving shadows
as she leans over the bridge rail
fishing –
Leanna by night light.

**Deep and Bright**

deep and bright,
vibrant in red -
the blush
from her face
stands in a vase
on my dining table:

Ms. Danuta's rose.

Rose

107

**I Have Watched This Rose**

I have watched this rose unfold
since Friday,
slowly every day from bud
to bloom,
and wondered at its beauty, its scent,
its vibrance.
I wish my life
had been as lovely as this rose,
its reds so deep,
its petals arching out to life
in rich profusion,
the most beautiful rose
I've ever been given.
It has helped
to heal
my heart.

**Why So Sad?**

Why so sad?
I was practicing Latin motion ...
And then what happened?
It broke.

**The Act of Dance**

The pressure
of his fingers on my back,
the urgency of his breathing –
they tell me,
command me,
move closer
move faster
move left
move right.
I follow a split second
behind his shadow
gliding over the ballroom floor
but I am so lonely
in his Prince Charming arms.
He pulls my body close.
I smile and
I cast up another wall
before my heart.
He is a remarkable young man
a consummate dancer and teacher
but I am not allowed to love him.
I do not want to love him.
It is all an act
a make-believe fanciflow
of magic and music and light
from which he could disappear
overnight
without a whisper of good-bye
and all I would have left would be
the memory of his thighs.

**The Slink**

After the Rumba competition,
a man among the spectators
said to me, "Wow, lady,
that's a lovely dress
you almost have on."
I smiled and flicked
my red feathered kick-pleat
at him as I slinked on by.

**Aruba Girl In Saucy Red Dress**

## A.K.A.

I have danced with you for years
traveled across the land with you
cared for you
prayed for you
hailed your successes
comforted your failures
I have seen
your children
born and grow
but I'm not sure
I really really know
your name.

**Upon Placing Second**

Upon placing second,
she said nothing-
but her
eyes
swore.

**When Trying**

when trying
to write a poem
about a rose
after all these ages
of poetry and lovers
   the shorter
    the better

**Dancing with Memories**
*waltz tempo*

in my arms
I hold this young man,
around the floor we go,
graceful, enchanting and lovely -
who he is I hardly know.
in my heart
I am dancing with Roman,
in my heart
I am dancing with Tim,
in my heart
I am dancing with memories
of husbands that yearly grow dim.
    Our time was cut short.
    Some blunder of life
    severed me from them
    but in waltzes and tangos
    I sweep 'round the floor
    dancing with memories of them.
I am sorry, dance teacher,
I make you compete
with men whom I loved
and are gone.
Some day in the future
when you too are old
and a young girl
in your arms you hold,
you'll understand me
and love's lost dreams
while the room turns in blurs
of music and words
while you dance
with memories
of yours.

*I have lived the American Dream*
*Thank you, God.*

## Acknowledgements

*With a Thankful Heart -*

*for Vern -*

In my mind, I see the created outcome.
Vern can figure out how to get there.
I get frustrated with computers.
They don't make my leaps,
the leaps I want from 0 to X.
Vern can figure out the technicality.
That's one reason why I feed him so well.

*for Vivian -*

My sister-in-law has been so encouraging.
Every time I mention the book,
she says she wants to buy it.
In fact, she says
she'll buy several copies.
I love that. She believes
without seeing.

*for Gabriel -*

Gabriel Sanchez, publisher,
the daring dude who volunteered
to coach an old pencil pushing wordsmith
into the Twenty-First Century
because she loved El Valle.

## Biography of Kathleen Bunyan Carlson

Kathleen started writing poetry at the age of seven and made writing her profession. She earned a BA in English, University of Wisconsin-Milwaukee; MS in Journalism, Northwestern University; and an MA in Creative Writing, University of Wisconsin-Milwaukee. She worked as a technical writer, grant writer and project coordinator for city and county governments in Indiana and Wisconsin, and for a technical college in Wisconsin.

She was born on the island of Aruba, Netherlands Antilles. Her family immigrated to Wisconsin in 1952. She became a U.S. citizen in 1974. She lives in Palmview, Texas with her husband Vernon who is a musician, painter in acrylic and watercolor, and nature photographer. His photos of birds and butterflies of the Rio Grande River Valley appear in Kathleen's latest book *Émigré*.

Publications include Foreword, *Border Arts: Beyond the Barriers,* anthology of The Raving Press; *Émigré*, Legado Publishing; chapbooks *Spiritual Reflections and Some Not So,* Westbow Press, and *Deep Night,* The Kenwood Press; selected poems published: on *Your Daily Poem;* in *Boundless,* the Rio Grande Valley International Poetry Festival; *Interstice*, South Texas College; *Flight, Fright, Mirrors,* and *Echoes*, anthologies of the McAllen Public Library Writers Circle; Ekphrastic Collaborations "What's Missing" with Angel Troyer and "A Scarlet Sash" with Heidi Hallett, Pewaukee Area Arts Council; selected poems, *Journey of the Heart*, Waukesha County Technical College.

Made in United States
Orlando, FL
05 January 2024